The Secret 8ᵗʰ Yahoo Reactions Book (Online Comm - entary)

Maverick Ashley Lenartson, Author

A\$AP Rocky trial: Trump sends hostage affairs envoy to Sweden in 'shameful abuse of office'

This is ridiculous on all sides. If A.S.A.P. Rocky was guilty do you think he would have paid the fine??? I think not. Our Illustrious President finally does something good and all you "NEGATIVE NANCY'S" can do is try to shut him down. The video of the incident should prove everything. You know how it is when you are a CELEBRITY: every last ahole on the planet thinks they can gain entry into your world. NOT TRUE: how'd you like it if you were in the middle of a tour and somebody tried interferring with you and you got into a scrap w/ some ahole half way across the globe??? You wouldn't like it. Then your tour get POSTPONED INDEFINITELY, etc. You wouldn't like it at all. Congratulations for TRUMP doing something like this. Most of you can go sit on something really big and YES, it's GOING TO HURT...

79-year-old woman sentenced to jail for feeding stray cats

I think the City needs to apologize to her and go after the person who left the cats behind. What is this world coming to??? This IS the Apocalypse right now...kindness is usually punished by stupid human beings...

'I can't describe a better father': Community rallies for grieving man who left twins to die in hot NYC car

He deserves THE DEATH PENALTY for a move like that. What kind of a parent forgets they have children in their car??? It's UNFATHOMABLE. PUT THOSE BRIGHTLY POST IT NOTES ALL OVER YOUR CAR, ESPECIALLY ONE where the key hole is for locking up the car that says: KIDS IN BACK SEAT. Change the colors regularly so that you don't get used to them. Nobody deserves to walk for FREE for doing something like this. I don't have children but I do know that IF I had children I'd be thinking about them day and night and making sure that they are alright. The gene pool is too shallow here. What kind of a parent does something like this??? I have no sympathy for what he is going thru. It's his own fault and the community deserves THE IDIOT AWARD OF THE CENTURY FOR RALLYING BEHIND HIM. They should all be SHOT.

Royal Caribbean passenger collapses in Florida cruise

terminal, saved by port workers

Hey, if you were on the Royal Carribean Line and just got off the boat you'd get sick too!!! Who in their right mind would want to take a Vacation away from home when some of these cruise lines dump their waste and garbage right in the ocean when they can darn well afford to put it in it's proper place...it's a shame that these multi-million dollar cruise lines can't act RESPONSIBLY!!! On, the other hand. congratulations for doing a wonderful job...

Report: Not enough evidence in near-hanging for hate crime

Where does one draw the line??? The boys clearly weren't thinking but they knew what they were doing: hate just doesn't spring out of places as it comes from your sick parents, the media and people in general who don't know better and never learned "no better". I was raised by two racists. It's not easy not using those words on people when other races piss me off, etc. It's like magic with those words wanting to come out but I do hold my tongue. Sometimes, I don't. Case in point my friend Michelle who is black who constantly blames white people for racism. Seriously??? She's part of the problem. I call it "Reverse Racism". I'm sick of it from both sides. I just want to get along peacefully with other people but that's just not going to happen with all the people who simply won't do it. Just the other day this black guy was starting trouble in Longfellow Square and asked me to shake his hand. I had already done so earlier in the night. I refused as I didn't feel like shaking his hand. It's like he was trying to run for office by starting trouble with people: then he says, "It's because I'm black isn't it???" I yelled at him and said, "Why the f**k do some of you black people always have to call out the RACE CARD when I don't want to do something with you???"

Then he started more crap with other people who were minding their own business. He ran away as he knew he'd get a beatdown if he didn't. Starting trouble in the middle of the night is no way to go. I'm just saying. Another black guy where I live, Roger, said the same thing, "It's because I'm black." I point blank told him, "That's not the reason. The reason is that you are an outright ahole and you constantly start trouble with people for no reason and then you wonder why they want to kick your a**." He didn't say anything. I left as I was too pissed off to deal with his b.s. anymore. These people exist. It's like they were born to drive people nuts by being "irresponsible human beings who spread hate and maliciousness and problems to everybody, not just white people." These days you do need a weapon just in case things really do get out of control. You never know if you could become the victim of somebody's hate filled ways. That's why a pen is a great way to thwart your attacker. So what the ink

Burger King's Impossible Whopper: Here's what eaters are saying

My Whopper is better than their whopper any day of the week as it's big and meaty and it fills you up...and, it doesn't need any preservatives to make it taste good!!!

Maryland family asked to leave Outback Steakhouse because son with special needs was too loud

Children with Special Needs who are Autistic need pine bark extract (pycnogenol) to calm them down so they can function like normal children. Of course, if the system did not give Antibiotics to babies and children w/ heavy metals like Aluminum, Mercury and other things in them they wouldn't develop Autism or other mental health issues in the 1st place. It is possible to inoculate with antibiotics that are not full of added things that shouldn't be there. You have to ask for that.

Middle school teacher faces backlash after handing out gender identity worksheet

Some of you people need to get over yourselves and stop acting like you come from Cave Man Days: on twitter there are 112 genders. It's not male and female anymore: not everybody fits into the dangerous category of male or female. Most of you people need to wake up to that fact and stop being "gender phobic". It just makes you look really stoopid.

'Teenage Dream' Co-Star Accuses Katy Perry of Sexual Misconduct

This is supposed to be news??? Why can't people keep their private lives PRIVATE??? I don't need to be hearing about it. So Katy Perry likes embarrassing men. What else is new??? He should have kept his mouth shut. It's not a big deal but he wants more relevance since his career is in total ruins rite now and even worse...who cares??? It should be the #imavictimmovement get over yourself. She embarrassed you in front of a bunch of people. It's not a big deal. Women are known for being k*ntz...they belittle men and wonder why some men can't stand them. That's what Society teaches. And, well, men are not supposed to come on to women. Since when is this??? I really don't get it. What a Society we live in. Bunch of sorry a** mo fo's. It takes two: he should have pulled down her bra to get back at her and in front of a group of people. Duh!

Man dies after competing in taco-eating contest at Fresno Grizzlies game

Will human beings ever learn that participating in contests that require you to perform human feats of action with your body will never work as somebody could get

hurt...when it's your time to go you might not know because you are caught up in the hysteria of the moment and winning the prize. Am I surprised??? NO WAY! R.I.P. Terrible way to go...I'd rather enter the hot dog sucking contest. No danger of getting killed there...or is there a danger there too??? I don't know...

Ron5 hours ago
The taco truck can now advertise; "Tacos to die for." Too soon?
ReplyReplies (44)
53389

MAVERICKLOVERin 3 seconds

Death By Tacos...who wants to sign up for this amazing contest??? The Prize: DEATH!!! Ron at least made me laugh. Don't care about why he said it: it's very funny...

Joe G3 hours ago
Taco bout tragic. Call 9 Juan Juan.

Trailer shows Lonzo Ball telling LaVar Ball that Big Baller Brand is 'demolished'

Hey, I need 1.5 million: anybody got that for me??? I'll invest the money...Promise to return it as soon as possible. PROMISE!!!

'Chrisley Knows Best' stars plead not guilty to financial crimes, released on $100,000 bond

Jizzley will do anything it takes to cheat the government out of money: most people would do the same thing. Human Nature. Who wants to pay taxes anyways??? He did the reality show so he could boost his clothing line brand and I don't know if it worked but airing his whole family's problems for all to see probably made him a ton of money. And, what does one do with that money: try to hide it from the government. If you are a reality star you better pay your taxes or you're going to jail. It has happened to the

1st guy who was gay who won the 1st season of Survivor, the guy from that reality show in NJ and many other people: wake up and pay the taxes as you're already a "REALITY STAR" and you're making $$$...no sense in being dishonest unless you have lawyers like Jeff Bozos does and pay 0 taxes on 67 BILLION DOLLARS...

Family of Dayton gunman apologizes for writing 'insensitive' obituary

When the funeral happens and the Obituary gets written people will always overlook the bad things a person did and try to remember the good in that person. It's Human Nature to do this. And, then in private people will talk about the kind of person they really WERE even if it's unkind talking between relatives, friends, and business associates, etc. That's just the way it is. HUMAN NATURE!!! We are all responsible for our actions in this life even if that means we end up dying because of them. That's life...Chances are it was the family that made him the way he became.

Police arrest man in attack on comedian Andy Dick

People attack other people not because of something that person did to them but because of past grievances with their parents, a friend, a relative, a business associate, etc. Has nothing to do with the person usually unless it WAS something you did do to somebody that caused them emotional pain & grief. It happens all the time. The trick is to avoid being attacked for being human. It has happened to me: broken nose. Did I deserve it??? Nobody deserves to ever be attacked for being who they are. NOBODY! To do otherwise means you are a miscreant who needs a victim...that's what happened here. There are too many people getting away with too many crimes. Don't let people take advantage of you as they will leave you high

**and dry after they get what they want out of
you and victimize you...no way to live...**

A$AP Rocky is found guilty but will not serve jail time

Ggddccbb 14 hours ago
What does that mean? I understand he was
found guilty and will serve no more time but is
it a something that will hinder him in his travel
or was there no other restrictions?
ReplyReplies (18)

664

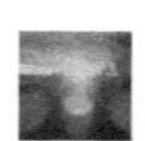

MAVERICKLOVER in 2 seconds

His travel will be hindered if the crime is
considered to be a felony and not a
misdemeanor. However, since he has been
allowed to keep touring he has been cleared to
travel but what do we know about any
RESTRICTIONS placed on his passport???
You'd have to ask his handlers. They'd know

what's really going on. Technically, he should not have attacked the people bugging him. He should have gotten away from them or called the Police to deal with the situation and since he is well known for who he is the Police would have shown up right away to deal with the situation. See what money can do for you??? It protects you from going to jail.

'I'm sorry, bro': Accused robber begs with armed guard and gets shot

Robo Cops love their jobs as this means they can get away with murdering somebody. I think that's how they get off...why is this so funny and why am I laughing??? Could it be the criminal pleading for his life and saying, "Bro, I'm sorry."

Body camera footage shows police officers pointing guns

at Yankees GM Brian Cashman

The Police have NO RESPECT for human lives: they're itching to draw their guns and shoot people: it's in their job description...Shoot To Kill...very sad state of affairs we have here in America.

Dayton contestant's eerily timed gun violence ballad is rejected on 'Songland'

You can't blame tRUMP or anybody else for your racist actions: he may be fueling them but he's not responsible for your tirades: YOU ARE!!!

A Florida man had 'a midnight rendezvous' at a construction site. Cops want him

Do we have anything BETTER TO DO here??? I don't think so. It's obvious the guy is fat and nasty looking but why go after people doing that??? It's not like he's stealing from the Construction Site in the middle of the night...cut him some slack. He should know better with people putting up cameras everywhere these days but come on...give the guy a break. Who would want that???

Sheryl Crow admits she saw 'strange' things as Michael Jackson's backing singer

I saw something strange, but I don't know what it was!!!

Emeril Lagasse laughs off Tommy Lee's complaint that he was kicked out of his restaurant

Don't think I'll be eating in Emeril Lagasse's restaurant any time soon as once again, The South Proved it has no class. Tommy Lee complied and said, "F**K,". So what. That's not a reason to kick somebody out of the restaurant. And, since when are you supposed to take your hat off in a restaurant??? Makes no sense to me...You don't diss Celebrities like Tommy Lee and his girlfriend. It only adds up to "BAD PUBLICITY" for Emerel and makes him look like a classless a**...remind me not to live in the South either. There are too many homophobes there stuck in the Bible Belt. Who needs that??? Uptight inbreds 'ya'll don't say...

CDC warns of 'alarming' strain of antibiotic-resistant Salmonella: What you need to know

Anybody with a brain knows that eating beef that is processed here in America or any other country and brought in isn't safe due to handling regulations and the processing of it with chemicals and then adding god knows what besides Sodium Nitrite or Nitrate to preserve it and make you sicker. You are better off and safer to buy meats that are labeled "ORGANIC" as these meats are not heavily PROCESSED and the animals are NOT FED ANTIBIOTICS, ETC. I didn't know that Sal Monella was so popular. I think he should just go away!!! As for drinking RAW MILK, the same goes for unprocessed milk from cows or any animal that isn't fed antibiotics and a diet that is not natural to that animal...that's the problem: antibiotic resistant animals from being fed too many antibiotics which makes them susceptible to the bacteria salmonella. Lesson over. Feel FREE to correct me if I'm wrong or make further dialogue here to open up the discussion...it's just getting started...

Madonna's 'Like a Virgin' stylist recalls scandalous 1984 VMAs performance: 'They tried to destroy her that day'

Special K1 hour ago
So many successful entrepreneurs -- and
that's what Madonna is -- step on the little
people to get to where they are, forgetting all
about them and saying "Me, me, me" when it
comes to their success.

MAVERICKLOVER1 second
ago
Special K. She didn't step on any people
except for her Security Guards making sure
she got what she wanted, etc. Can you really
blame her??? She's always been arrogant
and always will be. Has very little to do with
stepping on people and more to do with the
personality here...she's been known to throw
things back in peoples faces because she has
those little tantrums. Can you blame her???
How would you feel if people were trying to
get access to you because they thought they
were entitled??? It gets to you at some point
and you rebel...

I thought I was The Queen of Pop...what do you mean I'm not???
Woman Charged With Animal Abuse After Stuffing Dog in Car Boot

Some humans should not be allowed to breathe...

A Georgia attorney thought a man hit his Mercedes with a golf ball. He ran him over and killed him, DA says

Though I don't agree that he should have run the guy over and killed him I must say that, "...when you point your negative energy at somebody and make them a victim and they've done nothing to you ever, " expect that other person to get mad at you and want to kill you. It's to be expected...

Madonna's fans shut down 'haters' after 61-year-old pop star poses in sexy corset: 'She's in better shape than most of y'all'

Like a Surgeon, touched with the knife for the very 1st time, like a Surgeon, with your knife blade in body, whoa, whoa, whoa, you're so fine when you stick that knife in me and make me feel much younger, much younger, ohhhhhhhhhhh...something like that. She's had too many plastic surgeries and it shows. I hate her new album as it's got too much Autotune in it and in parts of the record it's hard to hear her voice as it's very muffled and I have to keep turning up the volume just to hear what she is saying. There are other issues with the record. I just don't like it and will not buy it. The album has about 5 good songs on it. The rest is filler...And, I am a Madonna Fan...don't even know if I can stomach hearing that record live at all...

UPDATE 4-Harvey Weinstein pleads not guilty, rape trial delayed to January

The guy is so ugly with that face of his how could anybody even consider letting him put his hands all over them. There's always the Option of RUNNING...I guess these women didn't think it through now did they...just because a director is powerful doesn't mean you're going to get the part. Maybe if some of these people got their mind out of the gutter...if there is No Police Report the judge won't be sympathetic to their story...he might even throw out the case especially if he hasn't eaten anything before getting on the job. Some judges are heartless creatures...they really are...

KFC is testing Beyond Meat plant-based fried chicken

I've got a BEYOND MEAT HOT DOG that is better than KFC any day of the week. So delicious. Anybody want to try it??? D E L I C I O U S!!!!!!!!!!!!!!!!!!!!!!

Kentucky Fried Dicken IS BEST!!!

In the face of death, the party of a life-time

I don't agree with this sh*t at all. He could have chosen to take Vitamin C to try to heal his Cancer and if that failed then maybe assisted suicide but I'm not a fan of it. Never will be. 3000mg of Vitamin C Organic is a great way to heal Cancer. Every other day. Otherwise, you'll be pissing it down the drain. One can also use weed or CBD Oil. There are a ton of cures out there if one bothers to look into them. And, HIV is a HOAX...it doesn't exist. It's the meds that kill you...people are so gullible.

http://whale.to/b/hiv.html I have no sympathy for what he did as he'll only end up reincarnating into similar circumstances to learn his lesson in that human body...

We can't just let them kill themselves: that would be too easy. The Multi-Billion Dollar Medical System needs to keep people living so they can make money off their dying carcass...Come On!!! Keep Them Alive!!!

_{U.S.}
Black man forced to kneel in boxers at gunpoint outside his home after police refuse to believe he is not a burglar

Dumb White Cops...oh yes they call it murder, murder in the 1st degree. He's lucky the cop had brains and didn't just point & shoot. Where do they get these cops from anyways??? The low end of the gene pool???

Oklahoma judge rules against drug-maker, orders $572M payment

Anybody with a brain knows that the FDA is the most irresponsible drug approving agency in the world. DUH, DUH, DUH!!! Get with the program folks. Killing people by knowingly giving them dangerous drugs is not cool. This country is one of the worst countries in the world: every time you turn around there's a medical commercial on the television for medicines that don't even work. What's up with that???

Current federal law says you must know English to become a citizen. So why are foreign language ballots even printed?

<u>Ashley Lenartson</u> **Because we love to kiss the a**ses of foreign people coming into this country and allowing them to help sink it deeper into a whole: after all, we are the "melting pot" of the world. Some of these people wouldn't be coming here if it weren't for some of the things we do to their country along with other countries making them victims because of our "foreign policies" that**

shouldn't be. We need to stop being "war focused" and focus on being PEACEFUL if change is to come at all...

TV star Jessi Combs dead at 36 after daring jet car accident

What could possibly go wrong attempting to set a "land speed record". My condolences. She predicted her own death from what she said. Very sad to hear.

Celebrity
Todd Chrisley's Son Surrounded By Family in Hospital: 'Not Today, Satan'

They will never go away until the network CANCELS THE SHOW: Reality T.V. pays too good, it really does. Drama, Drama, Drama... did this tip the boat over: we shall see. Great for more publicity. REALITY T.V.: That's what sells now a days. As far as being caught trying not to pay taxes, the Fed Govt. does it all the time: it's just that they do it without fear of being caught by the law as they are above the law. When anybody gets caught that's when they pay the fines, publicity, jail time, etc. If you pay your taxes you are good. If you don't you get a great lawyer and tax accountant to keep you out of jail so you don't have to pay any taxes.

Without This One Thing, Staying Debt-Free Is Impossible

Not racking up any more debt is the 1st thing to do: the government and credit reporting agencies already have you tied by the balls, etc. Why keep racking up reckless debt: it's to be avoided but when one can't even get past where they are as they're trapped financially "we have a problem." Millions of people are trapped in debt. There is no relief except to work yourself into your debt, watch what you spend money on and die in debt: rent, food, electricity, car, children, school, etc. Be careful what you wish for. You might just get it. Debt is a normal part of all our lives. We're just not taught about it growing up. And, when you reach an older age by then it's too late. If only somebody taught you to save 33% of your income as a youngster things would be different now...but, they're not. It all comes down to how you were raised and your parents not teaching you how to save for the future. You can blame that on them but you can't focus on that. Just keep an even keel and don't focus on what got you in debt in the 1st place...move along and be glad to be alive...

Alabama Republicans are urging Rep. Ilhan Omar's expulsion from Congress

The real Question is WHAT did she do to get herself in this position??? Does she have a right to be in Congress or is Congress supposed to be all "Straight White Males" with big fat bellies??? Does she have a legal right despite the fact that she is Muslim or does her AGENDA make it not so??? These and more questions need to be answered...I'm sure if I Google her name I'll get an earful with Ilhan Omar...I really will...but, can I believe what I'm reading??? That's the real question. FAKE NEWS vs REAL NEWS!!!

23-Year-Old Woman Practicing Danger-ous Yoga Pose on Balcony Ledge Plung-es 80 Feet and Survives

This must be the "Extreme Yoga" course I never heard about. You just can't fix stupid. Now, she's going to practice YOGA every day in her hospital bed after this kerfuffle...The Human Body has 206 bones and 270 at birth. I think she was trying to set a Guinness Book of World Records Record for how many bones one can break while trying to practice dangerous yoga poses and film them while doing it for Notoriety to post online. I think she's going to need a new brain after this incident. Now, she's probably going to have bone and muscle pain for the rest of her life...how stupid can one get??? I don't even like taking selfies and there's no way I'm ever going to buy a selfie stick just so I can get myself into more trouble. No Way! Maybe her next "stunt" should be doing Yoga Poses at the edge of the Grand Canyon. That should fix everything!

Tyler Skaggs another casualty of Amer-ica's opioid epidemic

Just because his mother did a great job of raising him doesn't mean he isn't going to fail: when you are a Celebrity for what you do you have a big responsibility not to get addicted to drugs of your choice: it's much harder to avoid because the limelight shines on you most of the time. He failed. She didn't. She did the best she could. But drugs, etc. are a choice. Just because somebody puts them before you means you don't have to take them. You can choose to walk away. Apparently, he had the kind of personality that falls for this kind of stuff. It's personal responsibility. No One Is To Blame EVER!!! He made the choices that killed him. End of Story! Very sad and tragic but one can choose to take the high road, not the low road. It wasn't an accident.

<u>911 dispatcher lectured woman who drowned on phone: 'I don't know why you're freaking out'</u>

When you are in a situation you can't get out of then you have to fight your way out. You can't rely on the Police or 9-1-1 to help you: just do the right thing and save your own life even if that means you have to break windows, try to open car doors during a flood, or mame people who are trying to harm you. Or, run...this is a tragic situation but most of the time it's too late by the time the Police arrive and you could have gotten yourself out of a tragic situation without their help...rely on yourself in times of trouble or better yet: don't get yourself into trouble. Rest In Peace Debra Stevens...

50 Cent Says Chris Brown Is The New King of Pop, 'Better' Than Michael Jackson

The only thing Chris Brown will be REMEM-BERED FOR IS being: The King of Beating Rhianna up and The King of Drama: everywhere he goes there's drama. He can't help that he is a "thug". Nobody can compare to MJ as there really isn't anybody as good as he was. He didn't seem ever to be able to overcome the emotional and physical abuse he suffered as a child from his father and mother (she enabled the s.o.b.) and never wanted to be an Adult. He admitted to that. Was not really capable of holding friendships with people his own age. Marlon Brando proved that when he started asking him if he ever did things with children and all MJ could do was start crying. When thinking about MJ you have to overlook the child abuse if you want to remember the good things he did while here and how much he really helped people with his singing and music. If only somebody had had the courage to intervene and really help him while he was still here he'd still be with us but not even his family wanted to try hard enough to do that. So sad. "We miss you MJ and wish the best for you." Some people just can't help but become trainwrecks. That's just the way it is: DAMAGED GOODS. But they're still good people??? I dunno on that one.

THE SECRET 16TH COMMENTARY FROM ONLINE YAHOO! ARTICLES

Maverick Ashley Lenartson, Writer to the Stars

Elton John Breaks Down In Tears As He's Escorted Off Stage Mid-Concert After Losing His Voice

If Sir Elton John has "walking pneumonia" then he's possibly on his way out as when a person of any age gets that especially when they're older it's a really bad sign: he should not be trying to sing if he's being diagnosed with "walking pneumonia" earlier in the day: he should be not performing and I don't care what his age is: he's not fit to perform and he's doing a "final tour" but how much is too much??? Walking Pneumonia can kill a person in no time at all. Don't take what I'm saying personally as it's not meant to be that way. These are just my thoughts on the situation. He should have CANCELLED the concert earlier in the day against the advice of his greedy managers and given the fans REFUNDS: it's really that simple. No need to tour if you're that sick.

Rosanna Arquette talks Harvey Wein-stein: 'I believe there are some Oscar winners who are not able to come forward'

- V The thing is, they own it sell it or trade it and still get to keep it.

- Maverick Ashley@V Everybody willingly sells their body for something whether they realize it or not: physically or tertiarily in this life: ultimately, we're all Prostitutes!!!

All-'American Idol' rejects: Wacky audi-tions steal the show on Season 18 pre-miere

Just listening to this makes me want to finish my project Makin' Traxx by Maverick Ashley Lenartson 10 Pure Pop Jazz songs that need to be finished in as little time as possible. I have 5 of them memorized and have to work on the other 5 and memorizing them. Two songs I'm going to strip down to bare essentials: Don't It Make You Feel Good In The Summertime & Dirty Girls & Bad Boys (Ode To Donna Summers). These are the songs I'm working on: 1. Crazy 2. Stone Cold & Crazy 3. Don't It Make You Feel Good In The Summertime 4. (Oh) Little Bo Peep 5. Pop Sensability 6. Together We Can Make It 7. Years Go By 8. Rock & Roll Cowboys/Rock & Roll Cowgirls 9. Sweet Satisfaction 10. A Girl Like You/A Boy Like You. These are all Top 40 Tunes as far as I'm concerned: I can see why people leave Maine for greener pastures as they can't find people to work with in Portland, ME. That's just the way my life works isn't it??? And, I'm considered Tone Deaf (Music Theory will cure that) and Atonal: so is Bob Dylan. Namaste! https://guaranteedtoop40pophits2016.blogspot.com Go Now...

Hollywood therapist Amie Harwick found dead: media

Amie Harwick shouldn't have put a restraining order on her boyfriend then allowed him back into her life: it's like trying to put sh*t back in your a** when you go to the bathroom or you let somebody who's been in your life GO...just let them go: she made the mistake of letting him back in. Who's at fault here??? I don't know. Ok, ok: Gareth Pursehouse, boyfriend, is to blame for...very sad indeed: she was a "Sex Therapist", huh??? Obviously she let a PREDATOR back into her life and this is how she chose to go according to Spiritualism. At least this is what Spiritualism teaches me: you just never know when it's your time to go: from what I'm reading, "...she should have put out..." but we don't know what they were arguing about but if he tried to assult the roommate then it's pretty obvious??? One can't ass u me anything here: so TRAGIC, isn't it???!!! She might still be with us if she hadn't resisted his demands!!!

She Didn't Want a Pelvic Exam. She Re-ceived One Anyway.

SINCE WHEN IS THERE ANY ETHICS IN MEDICINE: BIG PHARMA IS TRYING TO KILL AS MANY PEOPLE AS POSSIBLE W/ MEDICINES THAT DON'T WORK: Got any questions: ask your Provider what they'll really be doing to you and if you need to sign off on procedures that they'll perform on you when you're under anesthesia and don't know about them. They LEGALLY BY LAW have to tell you what they're ACT-UALLY DOING. The world is a very f'd up place to live in. Caveat Emptor: Buyer Beware!!!

George Zimmerman sues

Elizabeth Warren, Pete Buttigieg for defamation, seeks $265 million

Nayborhood Watch doesn't always turn out the way it should turn out does it??? This guys 15 minutes of FAME are already UP!!! Why hasn't somebody done something to him YET!!! S.C.U.M. of The Earth...I did read the story online but NO POLICE REPORTS. However, I do digress...I'm not asking anybody to do him in but come on...this guy is PURE HUMAN FILTH!!!

Elizabeth Warren skewers Michael Bloomberg, calling him 'a billionaire who calls women fat broads and horse-faced lesbians'

I thought Liz changed her name to LEZO now she's a LEZSBO and she takes a walk on the wild side for FFUN every now and then??? She should talk: a muzzle in her mouth would help...I honestly don't think this country is ready for Bernie or Pocha-heiney...I just don't think so...

Thomas L 3 hours ago
She's desperate as she's about to be voted off the island.

Maverick Ashley in 2 seconds

Elezabeth: please gather all of your money and belongings and GET OFF THE ISLAND BEFORE WE THROW YOU OFF…& take BERNIE WITH YOU!!! PLEASE, PLEASE, PLEASE…400,000 is a lot of money to teach how many classes??? Hmmm…

Bryan 3 hours ago
Bloomberg said in his defense it was only Warren he was calling a horse-faced lesbian.

Maverick Ashley in 3 seconds
Could she possibly be a turncoat as in turn those "mangled jangled blown out beef curtains over on the white plush rug???"

Franco 3 hours ago
Is it wrong to say it if it's true?

An almost literally explosive 'American Idol' episode: Gas leak leads to emergency evacuation

IF THE SET BLEW UP IT WOULD BE A GOOD THING!!!

Harrison Ford's Secret to a Happy Marriage Is Both Humble & Hilarious

The secret to A Happy Marriage: don't get married under any circumstances, see the person for a long time like 3-6 years and don't live with them before that time before you make a commitment to marriage and stay away from Addicts as they'll rip you off and leave you broke and busted. Is it HANDS SOLO??? Get It???

This Is Your Body On Red Meat

I recommend that Sexually Active People get as much red meat in their diet as possible as it will keep them ALIVE & HEALTHY! "You don't GO on a diet. What you eat IS your diet." Over consumption of food, especially, FAST FOOD is a problem in this Society since the 1950's: make healthy choices when it concerns what you eat: You want to lose weight? Take carbohydrates out of your diet, processed dairy of any kind unless it has ENZYMES in it, processed sugar drinks (even fruit smoothies from the store), meat is the HARDEST TO PROCESS BY THE BODY, any sugar products like cereal, sugary or salty snacks, no candy, no chocolate bars, and anything else that is causing you to gain weight and not like yourself. Also, make sure that you drink HEALTHY GREEN DRINKS that are not processed with artificial colorings, chemicals added that you can't even pronounce, etc. etc. twice a day. I could go on but I'm sure that enough people will hit reply in the replies section to counter what I say: more power to you. Namaste!

Ralph Lauren apologizes after using black fraternity

symbol on $334 chinos

I have a brown friend (not black) by the name of Michelle E. who was sitting with me in a restaurant called Bao Bao (Asian Food) recently (around Christmas Time) and she looked around and saw 99% white people in the joint. She then said, "What's up with all you white people who act so self-important." I said NOTHING as she doesn't like 1. (Black) Brown Men 2. Will only date Cream colored guys & 3. NEEDS to keep the issue or RACISM alive in my mind. Hmmm...I didn't need to respond to her NEGATIVITY. Everybody THINKS they're IMPORTANT. PERIOD. That's right, I'm YELLING in typeface right now... sometimes, I wonder IF I need to be her friend anymore. I'm just sick of "the blame game" going around and around and nobody knows when it's going to STOP!

Eminem reenacts Las Vegas concert shooting in new 'Darkness' video while calling for better gun laws

They took away all guns in Australia and I know of a friend there who says, "It's worked out just fine." Maybe he's the DELUSIONAL ONE??? I don't know. Look up "False Flag Operations" thru You Tube or your favorite music site: you will be surprised as WHAT IS REALLY GOING ON: it's all a calculated risk to DISARM THE CITIZENS so the government can take away even more of your rights...THINK ABOUT IT: I do believe in guns to protect oneself and hunt but some people shouldn't be allowed to own guns as they're too "trigger happy". Who decides these things anyways??? The Black Market EXISTS for a reason...where there's a will there's a way to get what you want/need these days. EMINEM is just trying to "cover up" his true feelings: the voting system is RIGGED...sooo...with that written HAVE A LOVELY DAY IN PARADISE, USA!!!

Celine Dion Speaks Out at Concert One Day After Her Mother's Death: 'She Was Ill for Quite a While'

CELINE was raised in a family that encouraged her to sing from a young age and there are other talented family members. It just so happens she is at the top of the pole and carrying the torch. She can AFFORD to fly back to Montreal, CA and be with her family: most people cannot. I'm sure that she'll be singing "My Heart Will Go On" as a tribute to her mother and all the family members who have passed especially her husband Rene. Not all of us have the opportunities that were given to her from such a young age but we all do THE BEST we can do with what we've got. Now, if she could just put on a little bit of weight that would be great: she has a dysphoria and I'm sure the passing of her husband is what did it...MJ and a lot of famous and not so famous people have the problem as well. At least she can still belt the songs out night after night...

Royal Caribbean says video shows grand-father knew window was open

Grandpa WAS an IDIOT: it's his fault, not the cruiseline: when somebody is doing anything they need to AWARE OF THEIR SURROUNDINGS: this is just a money grab for a family that has a "Stupid Grandfather". Sue HIM!!! Not the cruiseline...I'm sure the cruiseline is going to fight this tooth and nail and PROVE WHO IS GUILTY: NOT THEM!!! Of course, the "old, ugly man" has to live with this for THE REST OF HIS LIFE: it's called PAYING ATTENTION. No, I'm not sorry for what I'm saying: if more people paid attention to their surroundings there would be LESS ACCIDENTS: it's too late because a precious little girl was lost forever that sad day!!! I hope anyone reading this will THINK TWICE!!!

Aaron Carter Has Meltdown After Artist Accuses Him Of Ripping Off Work To Promote Clothing

Some of you people need to "GET OVER YOUR SELVES". Aaron Carter can do what he likes: do you think he really cares what people think of him making fun of Asians in a White Asian Voice??? Give Me A Break: anybody have a KitKat Bar I can chow down on??? I just took some Imodium AD so that I can Chill the F Out! HA! HA! Cultural Appropriation IS what it's called...I haven't even listened to his muzik so I can't judge...can any of us SNOWFLAKES judge him??? NO WE CANNOT...time to MOVE ON!

A Luxury Dish Is Banned, and a Rural County Reels

Ex-Grammy Chief Neil Portnow Res- ponds to Rape Allegations

I can't thank THE ACADEMY OF CON-ARTISTS enough for GIVING ME this #METOO OPPORTUNITY TO TELL THE TRUTH: The Court of Public Opinion IS NEVER WHAT IT SEEMS. It just ISN'T...I'd love to see the COURT DOCUMENTS: and, if it IS TRUE: "How much money will HE be paying out in the ALLEGED RAPE CASE???" Can I get THAT ANSWER on my desk when the time is CORRECT???!!! Doubt IT!

Aerosmith Drummer Joey Kramer Will Not Be Allowed to Play at MusiCares, Court Rules

Joey Kramer has ADDICTION ISSUES DUE TO ALCOHOL more than likely: that's why Aerosmith will not let him play: one has to remember that any band will replace any member when they cannot get the job done. Joey may not like it but that's his reality: maybe they have gotten smarter but I doubt it: it's the ADDICTION ISSUE getting in the way. If Joey cleans up his act then maybe they'll let him back in the band. I don't blame Aerosmith for doing what they're doing: they've been playing that GAME ever since they've been dealing with their own addictions in the 70's/'80's...think about that one...it's business as per usual. Carry On: no need to become a hater because you don't agree with band ethics...they'll do whatever it takes to survive even at the late state of their career. It's called BUSINESS.

Jessica Simpson recalls taking diet pills to lose weight at the direction of a music exec: 'I was down to 103 pounds'

The world tells us: you have to be pretty, smart, rich & young but when you get older you're ugly, dumb, poor and older: Hollywood places an unrealistic expectation on the citizens of America and when you can't meet that definition you're OUTTA THERE: hence, the botox, diet pills, face lifts and everything else it takes to make yourself look young even though your regimen just makes you look like a Two Panty Granny or Grandpa...why not just ACCEPT YOUR SELF AS YOU ARE! Isn't that SOMETHING TO ACHIEVE: F HOLLYWOOD???!!!

Let's hope startling courtroom image of Antonio Brown is his rock bottom

A lot of people are like he is...they don't think they have to pay their bills, can skip out on a restaurant tab, can get FREE rent, FREE everything, FREE money, FREE alcohol, FREE drugs, FREE MONEY FROM FRIENDS THEY NEVER PAY BACK, etc. etc. He had 10 million dollars: what happened to all that money??? Hmmm...it got spent...I'd be investing IT...

Jessica Simpson Shares Photo from Kobe Bryant Crash Scene: 'I Felt the Power in the Sky'

The BEST PART of Kobe was his ability to "dribble his balls". He was the best at THAT! I'm sure that his wife can attest to THAT! There are people who see things in the sky that you or I might miss. It's just a matter of timing and being Psychic w/ the eyes...but, I don't see anything remarkable w/ the pic taken of the crash area with the Sun's rays shining thru the cloud covered sky! Will somebody FILL ME IN???!!! R.I.P. PEACE ALL 9 people who perished early Sunday Morning...REST

Kobe Bryant's body, 8 others recovered from copter that lacked key terrain warning system

Everybody's a GENIUS at something even it means crashing a helicopter, raping children, stealing money from people who can't say, "NO," & "Go Love Your Self," cheating the system (gaming it), treating people like shit, eating bad food from a fast food restaurant, etc. R.I.P. Kobe Bryant, your daughter and friends who were riding in the helicopter with you. Remind me NOT TO BUY A HELICOPTER and to fly any winged instrument w/ my body as in paraglider, or even go skiing in the Winter or Summer, etc.

Yahoo Celebrity

Demi Lovato talks about coming out to her parents: 'I was shaking'

Until one has gotten their nose broken or been the VICTIM of a HATE CRIME then they can beatch all they want about their SEXUALITY: I'd prefer to stay in the closet as I'm not here to discuss my sexuality but I just DID. I know how JADED the world is and I live above a HOMOPHOBE who I took to court for 'Abuse and Harassment' and I lost the case (No Police Reports) but AT LEAST THE HOMO IS

LEAVING ME ALONE: we all know that IF you are AFRAID OF THE OTHER SEX you should at least try it ONCE to find out if you might actually LIKE IT/LIKE ME: then you can go back to your beatching and trying to CONTROL PEOPLE & weed them out of your life because you are a pathetic LOSER FROM SHELL WHO THINKS HE'S IN A GANG OF IDIOTS IN MAINE!!! --End of Sermon for Today 2020: may we all have the courage to be OURSELVES without feeling the pressure to do it...Ooh baby baby it's a trans world you can always get by (bi-) in a trans world.

Comedian Ari Shaffir issues statement on his 'vile' Kobe Bryant comments, says 'it's just a joke'

And why should I care what Ari Shaffir said??? He's an Adult, he can say what he likes even if that means there's going to be a huge backlash against him. Ari should know better than to make comments like that right after Kobe and 8 other people died in that helicopter crash. Now he has no Agent, no Agency, no Comedy Club to perform at because of death threats and people are pissed off at him especially Kobe Bryant's Fans, Family, The Media, and Everybody else including some of his fans who need something to gripe about, etc. His 15 minutes of fame are up for a while until people find the next thing to gripe about. What's a boy or a girl to do??? Forget about what he said, don't take it personally and move on.

Jay-Z and Beyonc sit during national anthem at Super Bowl

Entitled Wealthy People can do whatever they want: they don't care what anybody else thinks. If Jay-Z and Beyonce want to sit during the National Anthem at The Super Bowl that's their business, not anybody else's. It's not our job to judge them for who and what they stand for. Besides, Jay-Z owns part of the Super Bowl so he'll do exactly as he pleases with his wife, Beyonce & Blue Ivy, their daughter.

Atlanta Parents Left 'Overwhelmed' After All 3 of Their Sons Are Diagnosed with Same Eye Cancer

Some people even if they know they have a "genetic condition" will continue to have children no matter what: it's called NATURE. You can't stop people from having children but you can decide not to have children in this life. This is what I and my twin-sister have decided to do: 85% of the world is dysfunctional and raised in abusive conditions: verbal and physical abuse and that stuff seems to stay with us through our whole lives no matter how hard we try to get rid of it. It's indeed a very sad world. I come from a very sad, f'd up family but this doesn't mean that I have to be that way for the rest of my life. I can choose to overcome it and become a SHINING example of somebody who let go of his past and healed from it. Good Luck to those children/babies as they're going to need it. Apparently the mother didn't listen to herself before decid-ing to have children and now the problems she had are carried on to her progeny! So sad…what can one do???

The 'McMillions' Monopoly Scheme, Explained

McDonald's ISN'T REAL FOOD: if you want that you're going to have to pay for ORGANIC FOOD and that's double what the crap you buy with chemicals in it costs but worth every penny!

Marianne Williamson supports Yang's UBI but says 'it's not the second coming of Christ' for student loan crisis

The Whole System is one GIANT PONZI SCHEME: it's something one doesn't learn about until they graduate from College and by then it's too late. If one comes from a "Dysfunctional Home" then those unpaid loans add up very fast. I originally had around 15,000.00 in student loans in 1990. How does this equate to over 150,000.00 in 2019: oh yes, the INTEREST RATE @ 7-9%: the whole system is designed to bring you down from chemicals in the food, high interest credit cards, low checking/savings account interest rates, the stock market is rigged, cars don't last more than 10 years on the good side and rust out, the mortgage rates are higher if your credit report/score is low, etc. etc. The best solution: don't carry any debt you don't need to, don't get sucked into Credit Cards, etc. etc. Pay attention. At my age it's almost too late: this is exactly what the System wants: to sink as many people and straddle them with as much debt as possible. No way to live. Don't go to college: get Professional Help and Get A Job. College is a waste of time and money for most people as your degree is worthless when you graduate as you can't get a job in your field due to the competition, etc.

Rosario Dawson Is Giving Up Weed and Alcohol in 2020: 'I Want to Cleanse My Body'

Who Cares??? Do What You Want With Your Body...

Kobe Bryant tragedy caused Marie Osmond to reflect on her own 'devastating' death hoax

Jp36 minutes ago
Wasn't about her, so she made sure it would be.

Maverick Ashleyin 2 seconds
@Jp She's trying to make a point about death and her life and how Kobe's death impacted her life and how we should not take for granted living this life. Don't say things that will make you regret what you said is all she is saying. Make Amends where possible. Get close to people in your family if you can. If you can't make peace with them anyways.

LESSON: don't fly in helicopters unless you know what the weather is. Do yourself a real favor: don't fly in helicopters ever.

Shakira's Hit 'Whenever,

Wherever' Reaches No. 1 (18 Years Later!) Following Super Bowl Performance

I didn't watch the Superbowl as I'm not a Sports Fan and I could care less about most of the music that comes on the radio these days: One day you will be older, so be more grateful…

Newly released 911 calls highlight weather issues in Kobe Bryant crash

Well, maybe if the "Terrain Alert System" had been installed none of this would happen and how would Kobe know about it unless he was a smart man: anybody with a brain knows that if the weather is cloudy then you don't fly but wealthy people don't listen to anybody except their agenda now do they??? This all could have been avoid-ed…it really COULD HAVE!

Jay-Z Reveals Why He And Beyonc Sat During National Anthem At Super Bowl

People can do what they want and nobody has a right to say anything about it: you can't push the National Anthem on anybody. I knew a kid in grammar school: Danny Plourde. His religion [Jehovah's Witness) didn't allow him to stand for the National Anthem we had to say every day in Grammar School. So why should anybody force their opinions/views on anybody: it's a FREE COUNTRY: people can do what they want.

Science says Robert Pattinson is the most handsome man in the world

Here's What Andrew Yang Gets Wrong About Systemic Racism

Anti American

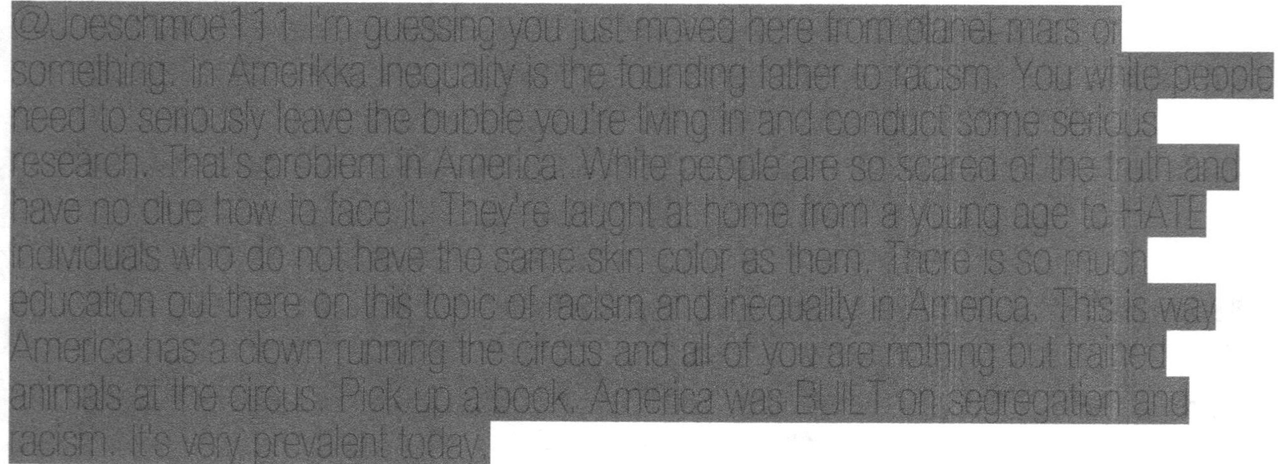

@Joeschmoe111 I'm guessing you just moved here from planet mars or something. In Amerikka Inequality is the founding father to racism. You white people need to seriously leave the bubble you're living in and conduct some serious research. That's problem in America. White people are so scared of the truth and have no clue how to face it. They're taught at home from a young age to HATE individuals who do not have the same skin color as them. There is so much education out there on this topic of racism and inequality in America. This is way America has a clown running the circus and all of you are nothing but trained animals at the circus. Pick up a book. America was BUILT on segregation and racism. It's very prevalent today.

• Maverick Ashley

@Anti American what's wrong with YOU NOT BEING ABLE TO SPELLCHECK what you write??? Is there something wrong w/ your EYES??? I SPELLCHECK everything before I send it out: are you losing your eyesight: this is an example of DISCRIMINATION: will you reply to me about it: here's my e-mail address: ashleylenartson@gmail.com You haven't provided one example of what racism is except for SKIN COLOR: you have to overlook the color of somebody's skin in order to get along w/ that person. Yes, you did well there but your Profile Name

Man arrested after allegedly driving van into GOP registration tent

Maverick Ashley 1 second ago
Now this IS the funniest thing I've seen all day longer: I'm VOTING FOR THIS GUY 20/20!!!

Elton John gets police escort, takes song requests at his annual Oscars charity gala

Michael 5 hours ago
Time for some truth. The Earth is BILLIONS OF YEARS OLD, NOT 6000! Dinosaurs were real & humans evolved from primates. NOT CREATED BY AN UNSEEN DEITY!!

Maverick Ashley now

@Michael Dear Michael, if we did evolve from Primates don't you think we'd look more like them??? We don't look like Primates.. According to Spiritualism we were created by "Creator Gods". Look that one up online. There is so much derisiveness because of the Creationism Theory vs. The Big Bang Theory. I choose to believe in Creationism. Believe what you want to believe. Humans were brought here and there were originally 7 pods of different kinds of humans, etc. That's what I choose to believe.

The rise and fall of Elizabeth

Holmes, who started Theranos when she was 19 and will now stand trial over 'massive fraud' in July 2020

RICH people usually get a FREE PASS because they have CONNECTIONS TO LAWYERS who will get them off the hook at some point even if that means the guilty party goes to jail for a while to make it look good. The little man or woman: SCREWED. Every now and then the Illuminati make a point about WEALTHY PEOPLE WHO STEAL, etc. and put them in jail anyways but that's rare. You've got to watch out for WHITE COLLAR CRIMINALS: those would be the Politicians, CEO's, Religious People in churches running big companies into the ground at the expense of the shareholders, or robbing money from the little guy or gal to enrich their coffers, etc. They walk away with millions and the company goes bankrupt and the public wonders what happened: it was GREED!!! It never really was about the worker's rights and treating them with respect and keeping the company in business.

Boondox 12 minutes ago
Did anyone ever sit back and say "This is too good to be true?" A sophomore dropout creates a revolutionary medical device in an industry with billions invested in research and development.

Maverick Ashley now

And what happened to the medical device that was created??? Was it useful or not???

Why Colin Kaepernick isn't playing in new XFL, according to Oliver Luck

Kaepernick has gotten TOO GREEDY with all the hype he has created protesting the

<u>Pete Davidson and Kaia Gerber Spend Time Apart amid Reports of a Split</u>

If she can't handle that big _ _ _ _ then send him to somebody who can…1. He's dorky 2. He's a CELEBRITY 3. He has a big _ _ _ _. 4. He's a talented Saturday Night Live Guy That's why women are interested in him.

<u>Adele's Transformation 'Was Never About Losing Weight,' Says Source: 'She Seems Happier Overall'</u>

One mustn't choose the 1st person they meet and fall in love with and get married: that's the number 1 reason so many people are so unhappy and get D I V O R C E D. Find out what your other half is like BEFORE you get married then you won't be disappointed. Also, not everybody is meant to get married. Some of us have life lessons to learn from being SINGLE. Marriage is just another way to hook people into the system to become miserable. Both parties must Communicate with each other in order to preserve the marriage vows. Otherwise, there will be two miserable people in a loveless marriage and two cold beds where two people sleep separately from each other. You don't want that. I've seen it happen over and over and over again. Don't let that person get away: work the marriage to keep the marriage. Then if there are children they're caught in the middle of the fighting all the time and 'Dysfunction Junction': you don't want that either. Work on the marriage or get divorced before children come into the picture.

A woman's side-by-side images show the reality behind the 'perfect' Instagram photo

BRAVE NEW WORLD: CAN'T STOP LAUGHING AT WHAT TECHNOLOGY DOES TO HUMANS...

TheWanderer 2 hours ago
Looks fade (or cost you a fortune to maintain long term), personality lasts a lifetime.

Maverick Ashley now
Some people have NO PERSONALITY & THEY NEVER WILL: that's the whole point of this article: VANITY KILLS - ABC

James Taylor reveals that he gave John Lennon drugs in the '60s: 'I was a bad

<u>influence¹</u>

WHO CARES: Just trying to "stay relevant" at his age: he can do what he wants and it's amazing what happens when one comes from a family that "coddles you" and makes sure that you will succeed in the field you choose to be immersed in and study all the time: when you're not "coddled" and you don't come from a "wealthy family" things end up terribly because of the way you get treated as a child/teenager: do I need to go into details: I do not: you want your children to R E S P E C T YOU??? Don't abuse them physically & verbally and raise the children EQUALLY & WITH RESPECT: otherwise, you're going to end up with DAMAGED GOODS: not a good thing to do to your children. Children shouldn't be SPOILED either: just makes sure that you treat them the way you want to be treated and that you encourage them to earn respect and that's with D I S C I P L I N E in everything they do. ENCOURAGEMENT all the way!!!!!!! !!!!!!!!!!!!!!!!!!!

<u>Ben Affleck says an associate warned 'you'll drink yourself to death' if he didn't drop out of The Batman</u>

Everybody has their ADDICTIONS: as far as Alcoholism goes, I'm lucky I don't drink anymore and don't and never really had a problem with it but when you mix alcohol w/ weed you end up on Probation for a year: that's the worst it ever got with me. As far as the alcohol goes: the body's addicted to SUGAR, not necessarily the ALCOHOL: replace the Alcohol with SUGAR/FRUIT

SMOOTHIES and then you won't be going through the D.T.'s after stopping your HABIT: alcohol kills 2% of the Population on Planet Earth EVERY DAY: so mind your manners and GET HELP IF YOU NEED IT. I had an Uncle Roger drink himself to death over a girlfriend (Lorraine) he split up with in the late 70's: it wasn't her fault: it was his decision to go into his Alcoholism that killed him and his taking PERSONALLY what happened. We all have out DEMONS INSIDE US WAITING TO KILL US: BEWARE!

- ReplyReplies (7)

Oraine 3 hours ago

I have a worse addiction than him. I'm addicted, for some reason- whatever it is, I don't know, to the Yahoo comment section! I'm here every single solitary day hours on end and I don't eat or even move when I'm on here! I'm on here as I wake up at four till when I leave out at work at 8 and then when I'm back from work at 5:30, I'm back here again until 12 to complete and restart the cycle!!! And it's even worse on the weekends!!!!

- ReplyReplies (1)

James 3 hours ago

Addiction is a drag. I'm addicted to cigarettes. I hope I can find the strength to quit soon while I can still breathe and don't have Cancer. It's my last demon I really need to conquer.

ReplyReplies (48)

Maverick Ashley in 2 seconds

Cigarettes are IRRADIATED by the BIG TOBACCO so you'll die QUICKER...buy ORGANIC as that will make you cut back seriously just because of the price and not

Need a New Driver's License to Fly? Prepare for a Real Wait.

Maverick Ashley in 3 seconds

VETTING & GREED w/ the licensing thing, huh???

We asked 12 climate scientists where they'd live in the US to avoid future natural disasters. Here's what they said.

70% of the population lives near the water and for a good reason: I don't know if there's any place that's FREE FROM NATURAL DISASTERS: it's just a matter of staying out of harm's way…that's what's BEST FOR BUSINESS!!!

Flat-Earther Daredevil Killed in California Desert Rocket Crash

I GUESS HE FOUND OUT THE HARD WAY THAT THE EARTH IS NOT FLAT & HE MISCALCULATED EVERY-THING. EARTH WINS EVERY TIME. https://www.goherenextoday.blogspot.com Get your BONUS today…go now…

Asia Argento, Ashley Judd and Mira Sorvino react to Harvey Weinstein verdict: 'The beginning of justice'

Maverick Ashley in 2 seconds
Well, according to some women: "Men are GUILTY of something even if they never did anything wrong." Should this have even gone forward??? Whatever happened to the "Statute of Limitations". In California it apparently doesn't apply.

jim 28 minutes ago
Will hollywood still include him in their awards shows and give him the standing O like they do for Roman Polanski ???????????

Maverick Ashley in 2 seconds
@Stephen The ONLY REASON Trump isn't in this line up is because he's THE President and it just gets overlooked and ignored as he has powerful lawyers preventing anything from happening...

'How many fathers are going to be inspired by Kobe's life?'

I hate to say it but, "If he had had any brains he would have used a different way to get to the event he was travelling to: he knew the inherent dangers of traveling my helicopter and should have travelled by car as he surely could have afforded it: it just would have taken longer to get there. And, he should have known about the issues w/ the helicopter as that's what SMART PEOPLE DO." Don't take what I'm saying PERSONALLY: it's not an attack of his good character: everybody has their flaws but he would still be with us had he used his brains. And, he certainly was WEALTHY ENOUGH TO BE AN INFORMED ADULT: now, because of this I'm going to keep myself SAFE AT ALL TIMES: Heed the warnings from this tragedy. Also, he's NOT A SAINT: so, we won't stop hearing about him and this tragedy for at least another year...such is life. I just won't be reading the articles, etc. R.I.P. Kobe, Gianna & Business Associates who died in this terrible copter crash. So sad...everything happens for a reason.

Hey, if I had a BIG _ _ _ _ I'd be cheating on my wife too. Just saying. That's how it is with people who can afford to have S-E-X with people they barely know:

'Curb Your Enthusiasm' star doesn't like when people jokingly call him Harvey Weinstein: 'a terrible, horrible human being'

Well, you know how some woah!men act when they're in HOLLY WOOD: they don't get the job because they won't supplicate to the "Casting Chair or Couch" and Harvey and this guy are so UGLY you'd have to put a bag over their heads just to think about doing them...sooo...nobody wanted to SPEAK OUT so they waited until the Statute of Limitations ran out and in Calipornia it never runs out: BEWARE OF WOLVES IN SHEEPS CLOTHING!!!

Teacher suspended over in-

class slideshow: 'I don't think they'd ever seen that before'

But, if you were PERCEPTIVE you ALWAYS KNEW who the possibly "Gay Teachers" were as you could sense it with your feelings: it's not something that was discussed openly like it is today but you JUST KNEW. I could name names but why bother? It's a PRIVATE MATTER ALWAYS.

Scientists discover Earth has a second (very tiny) moon

Camila María Concepción, Netflix Series Writer And Trans Activist, Dies At 28

SUICIDE IS NEVER AN OPTION: According to Spiritualism you'll only end up coming back in a similar body to finish out your existence as you FAILED at this existence. This is the ultimate form on meaness one can perform on their self. NO CAN DO! LOVE YOUR SELF. PERIOD. NO MATTER WHAT!!!

New York Times Editor Discovers Lady

Gaga's New 'Mystery Man' Is Actually Her Ex

Does anybody care IF Lady GaGa is dating her Ex- AGAIN??? Maybe they made up and liked each other all over AGAIN??? Why should I even care??? Now, when they break up AGAIN we're going to hear that reported all over the NEWS??? Is this EVEN NEWS??? It simply AMAZES me what passes for news these days. I like Lady GaGa and her music. Some of her MUZIK: she's looking like a Genie. Can anybody who's kvetching about her in this site of reactions say anything NICE about her instead of criticize her??? Hmmm...she can write songs, play the piano, arrange music on paper, dance like there's no tomorrow and can any of you do that??? Hmmm...that's called TALENT: people are sooo...JEALOUS these days: it just doesn't make any sense. It really DOESN'T.

Hunter Biden gets candid about battling addiction, says painting keeps him 'sane': 'The one thing I have left is my art'

Lynda 1 hour ago

Maybe it will help some people's mental health issues. Someone should suggest

Touch Me In The Morning, Touch of Grey, Touch Me, Touch & Go, Touched By An Angel, Sometimes When We Touch, Touch Too Much, I Touch Myself, U Can't Touch This, What I Said Was So Touching: Hunter looks a little bit on the raunchy side of things: when you're that rich is there ever really a bottom??? Daddy Don't Touch Me Like That...I sure could use 50,000 while I'm in a mental health rehab facility to make my stay so much more comfortable. I really could. Painting's not for everybody as the oils are toxic and can also catch on fire and then POOF! you're gone! That was so touching...tinyurl.com/jesussavedme Go Now...

There's a New Artist in Town.
The Name Is Biden.

I was addicted to crack for 4 years: red smelly crack. I'm still addicted so I go to Cawkaholics Meetings and have managed to taper off but every now and then I just fall of the wagon and get right back on after I satisfy my addicktions. https://www.tinyurl.com/jesussavedme Go Now: Buy Something Today& I'll send you a BONUS thru e-mail. 92% of my friends love my art. My friends love the fact that I'm an accomplished Well-Known Artist from Portland, Maine

Snippydad 42 minutes ago
The term "puff piece " comes to mind... Not ONE tough question?
Maverick Ashley in 8 seconds
His name's not Puff Daddy his name's Crack Daddy!!!

Helen Mirren says Meghan Markle 'was a fantastic addition to the royal family'

Megan Markle was similar to Princess Diana: The Royal Family just didn't like all the attention she got because she's NOT a Royal and she's an Actress/Publicity Hound: Megan & Prince Harry decided to leave the Royal Family & their duties as they'd had enough of being SHUT OUT OF THE FAMILY & THE Queen made it clear who was next in line for the throne and it wasn't them. That being said, "She's lucky she did exit when she did or she could have easily become another Princess Diana." You know how those Royals Operate, don't you??? These are just my thoughts: now, the Royals don't have to work w/ the constant INVASION of their PRIVACY, etc. It's what's best for business.

Ant and Dec's Saturday Night Takeaway gets 68 complaints following Pussycat Dolls performance

The SEXXY OUTITS were only a DISTRACTION TO THE JUDGES even though they weren't in any contest: it's just another way to get better ratings for a show like this. I thought it

was X-Factor I was watching but realized it's Sleaze Factor or
Sex Factor, not X-Factor. Oops! upside the head, I said, "Oops!
upside my head."

Justin Bieber Calls Wife Hailey Baldwin His 'Birthday Gift' as He Parties with Friends in L.A.

Cmo2 hours ago
They are both boys?

He's got a really big cl*t she likes to suck on and she has a giant
penis btwn her legs: they can't get enough of each other...

Elizabeth8 hours ago
are we just going to forget how he went off on her for beating hI'm at an arcade
game?
ReplyReplies (1)
1

Maverick Ashleyin 9 seconds
You know how it is when you've lived an ETITLED LIFE: you get spoiled and pull
tantrums when you don't get your way...
Reply

Elizabeth8 hours ago
him*

Wendy's breakfast sandwiches storm America: Inside the fast-food giant's $1 billion bet

DEATH RACE 3000: who wouldn't want a breakfast sandwich that looks like GMO EVERYTHING: I surely don't. SUPER SIZE THAT BREAKFAST SANDWICH: maybe my eyes are seeing DOUBLE. I dunno.
https://www.tinyurl.com/jesussavedme go now: buy a healing shirt today & feel better about yourself then go to Wendy's???

Fury as Kanye West hymn service pushes out transgender show

Mark 28 minutes ago

"I'll call you normal for not wanting to watch mentally ill sexual deviants..."

Maverick Ashley in 11 seconds

@Mark Mark just OUTED HIMSELF AS MENTALLY ILL: way to go! He's probably sitting behind the computer doing the crasterbation thing as I write these words...

Tripper 30 minutes ago

@Jeff

Why does god care where you put your willy so long as the other person can consent and likes it?

Maverick Ashley in 11 seconds

Recording Academy fires first female CEO, alleging misconduct

One should hire based on QUALIFICATIONS but DIVERSITY & EOE [Equal Opportunity Employment) are the norm these days but they come at a very HIGH COST: I'd prefer to hire somebody who's going to get the job done, not somebody who's going to throw me under the bus as they're a CONTROL FREAK & ADDICTED [AN ADDICT] TO POWER & MONEY HUNGRY: NO THANKS

'It does everything!' Upgrade to the 9-in-1 Instant Pot Aura for more than half off today on Amazon

Maverick Ashley in 11 seconds

Just because Yahoo! is FREE to use doesn't mean that some Corporation didn't pay for the advertising HERE!!! Think about it: there's such a thing as a FREE LUNCH but do you want to EAT IT???!!! Anybody who tells you, "...there's no such thing as a FREE LUNCH...," is lying to you: people throw crap out all the time especially in WEALTHY NEIGHBORHOODS and you mite as well take it on the run and be glad that you did...

Antonio Sabato Jr. on How Supporting Donald Trump Ended His Acting Career

From what I'm reading: 1. Has had drug problems 2. Had 3 different kids by 3 different women. 3. Needs more attention than he's getting as he's not happy being an "Actor"??? 4. Wants people to talk about him negatively because he's talking about how he got "blacklisted" recently and couldn't find jobs in Hollywood because he "PUBLICLY SUPPORTED TRUMP". I dunno. Maybe he's got "low self-esteem" and no matter what he does with his life he's "just not satisfied." From what I learned from a woman who taught me Graphic Design in the 80's: EVERYTHING'S POLITICAL: even walking down the street minding your own business & being happy listening to your Walkman, I-Pod, etc.

Fed cuts rates by 50 basis points amid coronavirus concerns

There are so many things you have to do to keep yourself healthy that I'm not even going to bother listing them here...Good Luck & NO FEAR EVER!!!

Dylan Farrow 'unbelievably overwhelm-ed' after publisher's employees stage protest over Woody Allen memoir

According to Spiritualism, "Dylan chose to go through this experience with her father." So what's the point of this "I got molested thing?" She needs to forgive the situation IF it did happen to her. There's no sense in dragging this stuff into the media but that's what families do when they're father is a famous director, actor and screenplay writer. The person who has been wronged needs/wants negative attention. That's WHAT THEY DO. I don't know the facts and never will. FORGIVENESS IS KEY HERE. Don't really care if it did or didn't happen. Neutrality. Things happen to you when you're a little child all the way to your teen years that your parents do to you that affect you for a long time afterwards: it's BEST TO FORGIVE THE SITUATION & MOVE ONE! According to what I've read all of our lives are based on things we did in our past lives: it's called Kharma - destiny or fate, following as effect from cause & Dharma - "cosmic law and order" & an aspect of truth or reality. We're all creating our own realities every day: sometimes it's best to Live In The Present Moments & Be Happy With That. You can't change your past: all you can do is FORGIVE IT! No amount of money can make what happened to you as a child better because the memories of your childhood will always be with you. It's best to remember the good times, not the bad times. Peace Be With You...and Dylan.

Oxnard10 hours ago
And yet the CONVICTED [no allegations, an actual CONVICTION in a court of law]
RAPIST Roman Polanski not only remains free but is often feted and otherwise
celebrated by the Hollywood elites and actors. It's these facts that COMPLETELY
undermine all of these unproven [unprovable?] cases that allegedly occur
DECADES ago…

Maverick Ashleyin 17 seconds

What is Consensual Sex in Uptight America??? A lot of Americans are mortified
with Public Displays of Nudity but not Europeans. Why is THAT???!!!

Stan9 hours ago
Roman Polanski is a bit more complicated than that. He originally was cooperating
with police. And he has made some great movies since then. To say that he got
away with something without repercussions isn't quite right, is it? And the girl, later
a woman, forgave him.

130CATHY10 hours ago
The sales will provide the protest. Just don't buy it

steve9 hours ago
If I owned the company my statement would have said something to the effect of :
We are a business and our decisions are based on whats best for our company .
Not emotions , feelings or public sentiment , As we require our employees to fulfill
their daily duties without walking off the job we have no choice except to find new
employees and terminate those who left our offices unattended .

Nothing New Under the SON3 hours ago
Problem with your stand is the people today WILL NOT accept sexual deviance.
Read what they found he did with all the other children in his divorce. That alone
should keep him from being published. GOOD FOR THE EMPLOYEES

Maverick Ashleyin 17 seconds
Then the company will have to hire all new employees if and when they get fired.
More work that doesn't need to be. People will Protest about anything these days.

Bill the Avenger10 hours ago

Remember no court ever found him guilty of any of the charges.

Maverick Ashley in 18 seconds

Anybody can and will say anything about anybody they want to that's negative just to bring that person down: that's how some people operate. It's a very sad world that we live in. Now, if people could just mind their business and do the right thing wouldn't this be a better planet?

Maverick Ashley in 17 seconds

What is the true definition of the word PERVERT? noun /'pərvərt/ a person whose sexual behavior is regarded as abnormal and unacceptable. Ex. homosexual, cheating in your marriage, a person who has sex with underage children or teenagers, a man or woman who gets off on exposing themselves to people using an overcoat. The list goes on from here.

Why Isn't SXSW Canceled Yet? It May Come Down to Insurance and the City

The festival should go on as planned as it brings a lot of revenue to the city? WIN/WIN Situation. Doesn't matter IF you like the bands or not. It's called MUSIC. We're living in the 'Age of Enlightenment,' aren't we??? Yeah right. Either you go to the Music Festival or you don't. Problem solved.

Amanda Bynes's fianc confirms that they've ended their engagement

It all depends on how you're raised: at some point you have to LET THE PAST GO and move on with your life: some of us want to remain children because of the mental and physical abuse. The "Emotional Pain Body" will stop you out from becoming a successful person. You have to honor your self every day that you Live

<u>Nigeria is already dealing with a deadlier viral outbreak than the coronavirus epidemic</u>

Who wants an OPEN BORDERS or THEY'LL GET HERE ONE WAY OR ANOTHER shirt???

<u>Celine Dion Styles Michael Kors Ensemble with On-Trend Knee-High Boots</u>

If you lost your husband when he was 73 you'd probably react the way she's reacting. She has a "body image" problem: it's called Dysphoria. MJ had the same issue and disfigured his face because his father and siblings called him "Big Nose" while growing up. It changed him forever. Same thing with Celine: she's just not gotten over the death of her husband Rene Angelil. Sad, but, that's the way it is...but, she can still sing like no other singer if that's the kind of music that you like.

<u>Harvey Weinstein fell and hit head while in jail, is reflecting on past behavior, rep says</u>

I'm a SEX OFFENDER: I look at both sexes and they get offended. If I was him I'd be doing the same thing: coming up with any excuse to avoid Riker's Island and end up in the Hospital where I'll be MUCH SAFER. You would, too!!! https://tinyurl.com/jesussavedme Go Now: tell US what you bought today! Support The Artists/Arts in Portland, Maine

Maverick Ashleyin 1 second

I'll take the FOOTLONG: I'm horny.

Maverick Ashleyin 1 second

I'd rather pay for sex: Quid Pro Quo: I give you something and you give me something. Problem SOLVED!!!

Nikita Dragun Wore a Thong Over Her Pants and It's Going to Take Me Several Days to Recover

Everything about her looks fake especially her boobs: Welcome To Trans 2020...Thank You very much.

Maverick Ashleyin 5 seconds

I'd rather lick something else: dear readers can fill in the details.

Maverick Ashley in 5 seconds
#thebuttholechallenge

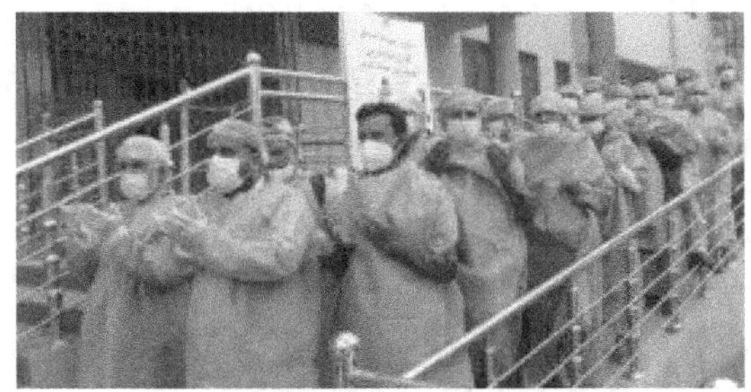

Florida man whose 'game changer' coronavirus treatment was touted by Trump is a believer, but warns: Don't try this at home

BEFORE YOU DO ANYTHING ALTERNATIVE DO A COMPLETE [INTERNET] SEARCH OR OTHERWISE TO FIND OUT THE EFFICACY OF WHAT YOU'RE TAKING TO HEAL YOURSELF: YOU'VE ONLY GOT YOURSELF TO BLAME IF YOU MAKE YOURSELF SICK & DIE: INVESTIGATE IF WHAT YOU'RE DOING IS SAFE & THE SIDE EFFECTS!!! OVER & OUT!!! ALL CAPS FOR A REASON...

Kathy Griffin: I Was Sent to ER Corona- virus Isolation

Room With 'Unbelievably Painful Symptoms'

She's an EXAMPLE of what TOO MUCH PLASTIC SURGERY does to you: it ruins your looks: she could have tried something Organic & Natural like Olive Oil, Coconut Oil or something else that wouldn't ruin her looks...TRY AGAIN!

Seth Rogen discovers 'hilarious' Amazon Alexa feature: 'You're doing God's work'

Alexa, can I hear a Donna Summer fart??? "Toot toot aye, beep beep, toot toot aye, beep beep."

Lee5 hours ago
This is what people with money sit around and do...im getting my garden ready to plant.

Maverick Ashleyin 6 seconds

This year I'm planting only flowers in my Empty Garden for John Lennon & Elton John. I'm sooo...PROUD of my elf...he's going to help me git 'er done...

Mississippi Governor Creating 'Mass Confusion and Panic' Amid Pandemic

Barryyesterday
All the states bordering Mississippi should put up barricades along the state border

with Mississippi so no one can leave and get into their state.

I know this violates a constitutional right to travel, but constitutional rights can be abrogated when faced with an issue of genuine state interest. There is no question but that the coronavirus crisis is exactly that. A state has an important interest in protecting the health of his citizens. Since Mississippi is acting irresponsibly and dangerously, this will limit the harm to it's own geographical borders. I would not let one person past a state line out of Mississippi. It's as simple as that.

jojo 3 hours ago

They should have done that years ago, Mississippi is the most ignorant /dumbest state in the USA, 90% of them can't spell Mississippi

Maverick Ashley in 8 seconds

@jojo if you're DUMB that's YOUR OWN DOING: don't need to spread the blame further than it already goes…

Chip 8 hours ago

@nino Trust me Tate Reeves is a #$%$ joke, problem with Mississippi is there are only about 3 million folks living here, out of the 3 millions only about 800,000 people vote........About a million people are to young to vote and the other 1.2 million feel so disenfranchised they just stay home........Mississippi is a great State lots of good folks problem is the majority of the 800,000 that vote can?t think outside the box cause they keep voting for the same clowns to run the State and it shows by Mississippi being dead last! I?m very conservative but I will continue to throw my vote away to the independent candidate instead of giving it to the republicans until we have Term Limits in all State and Federal elected officials!

Maverick Ashley in 8 seconds

@Chip THESE STUPID POLITICIANS WOULD NEVER ALLOW "TERM LIMITS" as

Conor McGregor calls for military to enforce Ireland's coronavirus shutdown

Of course he can afford to say this to the media: he's a Media Whore and he's got so much money that this whole Quarantine thing really doesn't affect him as he can hide behind closed doors and do what he wants to do and keep himself safe...IDIOT!

IRS releases more info on how to get coronavirus stimulus checks ASAP

THE IRS CHANGES THE TAX CODES AND RULES EVERY YEAR TO CONFUSE PEOPLE AND RIP THEM OFF MORE FOR NOT BEING ABLE TO FOLLOW THE DIRECTIONS & RULES: IT'S IMPOSSIBLE WITHOUT A GOOD TAX ATTORNEY OR SOMEBODY LIKE THAT. OR, YOU CAN FOLLOW THEIR B.S. TO THE T!!!

Biden and other Democrats blast Trump's health care rejection amid coronavirus

Is it the Corona Virus, The Coronavid-19 virus or the Coronassallingus virus: just asking for a friend who's em bare ass ed to even ask that word: can anybody pronounce it??? That was a joke, a joke: https://www.toolsforfreedom.com to learn

more about what's REALLY going on with this manufactured
virus designed to put the whole world on lockdown...go now:
edjewcayte urself...I'm totally SERIOUS...

Elected officials shouldn't be able to own or trade stocks. Period.

VERY TRUE because of INSIDE INFORMATION - Foreigner
sang about it a long time ago...https://toolsforfreedom.com to
learn more about Corona Virus and what's really going on...

Coronavirus could wipe out department stores: former Apple store chief

THE #1 reason Big Giant Retail stores go BANKRUPT: CEO's
take a 57 Million Dollar Pay Raise and the employees work for
minimum wage: whatever that is in your area. PROFIT
SHARING IS THE WAY TO GO. Everybody WIN/WINS.
Then there's the fact that the stores are franchises which means
more Inventory & Overhead, etc. etc. Then one has to deal w/
the part as an employee not being able to work more than 32
hours per week, etc. If you want to buy something online buy it
2 sizes bigger than you need as anybody who's been thru this
experience knows that Asians are smaller than Americans, etc.
so you're going to get fkd when you buy something made by
them and a Large shirt won't fit a really big guy. That's why
there are L shirts that are smaller like a medium or a L or XL,
etc. I won't even go into women's clothes: but you can figure out

how big to buy for a man, etc. if he's into that kind of thing...the sizes transfer: there's a chart online that will show you that...has the Internet destroyed Humanity as it once was or it's much easier to sell on than offline: all depends on what kind of a person you are: when you order online you have to wait 1-3 weeks for delivery depending on the company and if you go to a Mall then you can try it on: otherwise, don't buy it...you might be wasting money by not trying it on for size and fit, etc. Everybody wants everything YESTERDAY anyways and that's no way to live your life...Live In The Present Moments...that's all one can really do.

Toilet paper shortage during outbreak? Here's why

WIPED...OUT!!! WHAT HAS THIS WORLD COME TO??? https://www.goherenextoday.blogspot.com go now: I'll tell you a story about my 1st experience using toilet paper and what happened...

Disney Shared Its Famous Churros Recipe—And You Probably Have All the Ingredients

Any flour that's not loaded with gluten: try a flour that's not loaded with any gluten like Buckwheat, Rice or Quinona Flour: there are a ton of them out there. Your bones and muscles will thank you for this later. Sugar is also a culprit. Got to watch out for flour and sugar: deadly combination.

Op-Ed: Coronavirus pandemic hoarding pushed me to give up toilet paper

Mariel Garza
Los Angeles Times Opinion

Maverick Ashleey Lenartson

I ran out of toilet paper so why hoard? Just use a washcloth: no
more wondering when the toilet paper's going to run out and
thinking, "OMG, I've got to rush to the store right now or I
don't know what I'm going to do."

Alison Brie says training for 'GLOW' helped her battle with body dysmorphia: 'It took the motivation out of being skinny'

Chau 17 hours ago

I'm glad I've been ugly my whole life and learned to accept it early on

MAVERICKLOVER 1 second ago
Some of the UGLIEST people in the world are BEAUTIFUL!!! Put that in your pipe and smoke it. UGLY IS THE NEW BEAUTIFUL

old guy 17 hours ago
"Lord my body has been a good friend
But I won't need it when I reach the end"
Cat Stevens

Spiflecheck 19 hours ago
Body dysmorphia is not concern over weight and body image, it's a serious condition where someone believes an otherwise healthy body part isn't, to the point where they seek to damage or remove it. Celebrities hi-jacking that term so they can have a "condition" is ridiculous. She works in an industry where appearance is king, which causes angst I'm sure, but not "body dysmorphia".

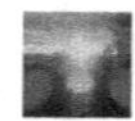

MAVERICKLOVER in 3 seconds
Michael Jackson, Pattie LaBelle, Celine Dion: the list goes on of famous and not so famous people. Look at what MJ did to himself and Celine just looks like The Scarecrow: it's very

disturbing to see her in concert and have to think about it thru the whole concert: Celine can still sing like never before but the look isn't to healthy to look at.

'We are dead': People with disabilities fear they will be on losing end of doctors' life-or-death choices amid coronavirus crisis

Gloom & Doom is what I'm hearing: it's not as bad as you think: people who are taught how to hunt & kill will be the ones who survive if Society ever falls the way foreign countries fall because of the interest rate on their dollar bills, etc. If a person has a auto-immune disease, etc. they can use COLLOIDAL SILVER to stop the spread of their disease: everybody has lessons to learn in this lifetime: people who are disabled are no exception to any rules. Some of US have "disabilities you can't see w/ the naked eye". Mental Health Issues...

Rob n Oregon 7 hours ago
As a disableg citizen with congestive heart failure, an enlarged heart and multiple organs working improperly I have to say I am not worried in the least bit. I have long out lived the assumption of the heart specialist who said go home and make a will 8 years ago , I have lived thru childhood aids, sars, the bird flu, the swine flu, sars and god only knows what other pathogens I have came in contact with when I was able to work. If it is my time to go then there is no amount of worry, crying or shaking my finger that will change a thing, when your time is up it is up period. What worries me is the financial end of it, the panic buying by people has put those on disability in a bad position because all the less expensive item are bought up by people who get money more then once a month. This leaves the disabled forced to go out multiple times to be able to complete their shopping on the budget they have to shop if they can find items they can afford and increases their chances of coming in contact with those who are exposed to the virus.

MaverickAshley just now
Like the Ma Bell commercial says, "Call before you come."
That includes buying stuff at the Supermarket: no need to go out
if you think ahead of schedule. Order thru an online service.
That's what I do when I get lazy.

Sunlight destroys virus quickly, new govt. tests find, but experts say pandemic could last through summer

Go to https://www.toolsforfredom.com to find what's REALLY
going on w/ this Corona Virus B.S. Then you'll know what the
government IS really up to...until then, you'll be in the dark with
everybody else who doesn't know how to become EDUCATED
ON THEIR OWN ABOUT THIS MESS & who relies on the
MEDIA and their disinformation campaign...just sayin'...

Lori Loughlin judge disturbed by defense allegations of misconduct in college admissions scandal

Here's the thing: Lori Laughlin had enough money to pay for the

girls' college but not enough smarts to NOT pay somebody hush

money to get them in: they could have gotten in on their own merits and had a wonderful life at USC w/ mama's and daddy's purse strings but she had to choose the ILLEGAL METHOD: what's wrong with this woman??? I'm not the only one who sees this: A cushy life: let the girls get admitted to USC on their own merits, get in and then sail thru 4 or more years on the coat tails of the parents: how hard is that??? Apparently VERY HARD. I don't think HONESTY runs in this family: Money CORRUPTS some people. They whole family must be feeling VERY DUMB by now or maybe it just didn't register YET???!!!

Watch Steve Perry Deliver a Stunning Quarantine Rendition of Beach Boys Classic 'In My Room'

Steve Perry's problems w/ the band started when he had hip injury while hiking and he didn't want to continue on with the band so they made the decision to carry on without him: besides, his singing days and hits were behind him in the late 80's so he CHOSE not to carry on with the band. Nobody can be blamed as some people are trying to place blame HERE: he's doing what he wants and the reason people are pissed off is because he won't go back to the band and that's for personal reasons: if that accident had never happened when he went hiking he'd still be touring. Maybe. Same thing with Michael Jackson: if he had never had that Pepsi Commercial accident and his hair caught on fire burning his scalp would he have become a drug addict??? I don't know. Probably because the doctors turned MJ into a Science Experiment. Either way, MJ and Steve Perry are responsible for what happened to them. Nobody else.

Will There Be A Meat Shortage Because Of The Coronavirus?

YES, THERE'S A MEAT SHORTAGE: I'M NOT GETTING ENOUGH MEAT IN MY SEX LIFE. PLEASE, SOMEBODY HELP ME TO OVERCOME THIS SHORTAGE. I NEED MEAT TO KEEP ME GROUNDED, SATISFIED & HAPPY!

Shark Tank 's Daymond John Denies He Tried to Sell Masks at Inflated Prices to Florida amid Coronavirus

I WISH I WAS A MILLIONAIRE AND COULD BUY SOMETHING AT WHOLESALE AND THEN TURN AROUND AND MAKE A HUGE PROFIT SELLING: BUT, IT COMES DOWN TO ETHICS: WHEN YOU REACH THE LEVEL HE HAS REACHED DO YOU MAINTAIN ETHICS OR DOES GREED KICK IN. IF PEOPLE, CORPORATIONS, THE GOVERNMENT, ETC. ARE DUMB ENOUGH TO BUY THE MASKS, HE DESERVES TO MAKE A PROFIT. IT'S A FREE WORLD OUT THERE: DO WHAT YOU WANT BUT BE CAREFUL WHO YOU RIP OFF OR FOOL ESPECIALLY

IN THESE TIMES. https://goherenextoday.blogspot.com go now...

Doctors warn against vitamin drips, Clorox baths after Cristina Cuomo touts them as coronavirus treatment alternatives

Anybody who wants to know more about "bleach + old timer remedies" and vitamins & minerals taken 2X a week should do a search about that EXACTLY! Then you will know more than you did 10 minutes ago: bleach is a non-causative agent which is very anti-viral when used in bath water: 2 teaspoons + two teaspoons of lemon, lime or orange juice to neutralize the minerals and the chemicals in the water that shouldn't be there. You have to sit in the water for at least 20 minutes to let the water + bleach + lemon to get into your body and clean it out of anything that shouldn't be there. Ex. Covid-19 Virus, etc. And, you have to do this healing for at minimum of 2X a day for 30 days for it to have any effect at healing your body. I'd know from the things I've done with my body in my lifetime. Ex. I used shiitake mushrooms drunk as a very strong tea for 120 and got rid of herpes. No more outbreaks anymore. Anybody who uses their brain should know that you are never supposed to drink bleach as it will ruin your esophagus and you'll have to go to the hospital. More than likely you'll die on the way to the hospital as bleach is an agent that has Antimicrobial efficacy The broad-spectrum effectiveness of most bleaches is due to their general chemical reactivity against organic compounds, rather than the selective inhibitory or toxic actions of antibiotics. They irreversibly denature or destroy many proteins, making them extremely versatile disinfectants.

Hypochlorite bleaches in low concentration were also found to attack bacteria by interfering with heat shock proteins on their walls.[15] One should always think things through before they do them in the 1st place. Then you'll be better off in the long run: make a plan and stick to it. Health hazards
The safety of bleaches depends on the compounds present, and their concentration. Generally speaking, the ingestion of bleaches will cause damage to the esophagus and stomach, possibly leading to death. On contact with the skin or eyes, it causes irritation, drying, and potentially burns. Inhalation of bleach fumes can damage the lungs. Personal protective equipment should always be used when using bleach. Bleach should never be mixed with vinegar or other acids as this will create highly toxic chlorine gas and can cause severe burns internally and externally.[35][36][37][38] Mixing bleach with ammonia similarly produces toxic chloramine gas, which can burn the lungs.[35][36][38] Mixing bleach with hydrogen peroxide results in an exothermic chemical reaction that releases oxygen, and may cause the contents to splatter and cause skin and eye injury. Heating bleach and boiling it may produce chlorates, a strong oxidizer which may lead to a fire or explosion. Fraudulent product Miracle Mineral Supplement, whose main active ingredient is sodium chlorite, is sometimes dangerously promoted as a cure for a wide variety of health conditions.[39]

Peter Frampton tells how David Bowie carried him from smoking plane

I've still yet to meet the man or woman of my dreams who

carries me out of a smoking plane before it catches on fire! What a beautiful story this is. How long was it before David proposed to Peter??? I didn't know they got married. Or, did Peter just say, "I'm not that way!" Then with a smile Peter said, "David, you can have me anytime you like." Said with a hint of snickers and sarcasm galore!

Mike Tyson Offered More Than $20 Million to Fight Again in Single Match

Longtime public defender on Central Park video: 'The cops are inclined to believe a white accuser and the other person gets arrested.'

Maverick Ashley in 1 second

@Kaboom People FORGET what he did: I forgot: who was it again? And, was it true???

Maverick Ashley in 5 seconds

I had an American Indian woman doing this to me & I'm cream

colored (i.e., white): constantly calling the cops and making false accusations saying I was "harassing her" (got arrested 4 times, had to pay to get out of jail, report never went anywhere) and I'd get arrested and I'm white/cream colored: it goes BOTH WAYS: people make up stories to get somebody ARRESTED because they're VINDICTIVE LITTLE BEATCHES: A FALSE POLICE REPORT should require: 1. 1000 fine 2. 30 days in jail 3. Name in the paper: but does this happen all the time??? IF people got FINED for making FALSE POLICE REPORTS this stuff would stop but does the system do its job? NO WAY! PEOPLE NEED TO STOP BEING STUPID & ACTING LIKE VICTIMS: TAKE RESPONSABILITY FOR YOUR FEAR: GROW UP!!! I'm saying this from a male's perspective. Women have all the rights in "Society" so they can do whatever they want. After all, Society made up all these rules for men and women to follow so they must be right??? Doubt It!!! SOLUTION: to get along with a person who isn't your skin color??? Overlook that "issue". Just stop being racist/using skin color as an excuse to f with somebody: it's just not correct.

Kylie Jenner is reportedly no longer a billionaire, and Forbes says she likely showed it fake tax returns: 'It's clear that Kylie's camp has been lying'

I'm a BILLIONAIRE: will somebody please go to my website and buy something today??? More like a DOLLARAIRE: goherenextoday.blogspot.com to buy something that puts a

SMILE on your face...go now...

Why do all hot dogs look alike? They're in bread

Rock & Roll All Night & Party Every Day

Khloe Kardashian finally addresses her dramatically different look: 'Once and for all stop doing it'

She looks like a sex crazed obsessed blow up doll who pouts her lips too much. Everything has to be PERFECT with her: I can see another reason people are sick of this family: too much money and too much time on their hands.

Pink Wants People to Stop Saying 'All Lives Matter' — & She's Right

"ALL LIVES MATTER" DEPENDS ON HOW YOU THINK ABOUT IT: IT'S TRUE: ALL LIVES DO MATTER, NOT JUST THE PERSON WHO SAYS IT: THAT'S THE POINT OF SAYING IT: HAS NOTHING TO DO WITH ME BEING DEPRESSED, SAFE, ETC. I THINK SHE HAS IT ALL WRONG & SHOULD JUST SHUT UP: I'M NOT GETTING WHAT SHE'S SAYING!!!

Man gets $1.1 million bill after surviving 62 days in hospital with coronavirus

I won a million dollahhs and I can't believe I received a bill from the I.R.S. How rude. This country is the battle ground for the world and not much wiser for what's happening in this country right now. Such a shame. https://goherenextoday.blogspot.com today: go now...

Cup Foods, a Minneapolis Corner Store Forever Tied to the Death of George Floyd

B.M.M. Bowel Movements Matter: I always feel so much better after a good bathroom break. Don't you??? https://goherenextoday.blogspot.com buy something that contributes to the growth of humanity.

Aunt Jemima to remove image from packaging and rename brand

Why not just make a white version of Aunt Jemima or will that be considered racist as well??? People are taking this crap too far: innocent black, white and all races are killed by the Police every year: they're trained to kill: that's their job: if you brandish anything that looks like a weapon you're DEAD: that's the lesson here: some people just don't realize this. When you're stopped by the Police just 1. Cooperate 2. Don't run or show anything that looks like a weapon 3. At some point you can ask them: Am I FREE to go when they keep deposing/holding you and you don't know why. If you do know why don't give them any information. It's in your best interest, not theirs. 4. Get away as fast as you can once you're cleared of any wrong doing. Keep your "nose" clean and don't do anything else to get them speaking to you again: there are alot of crazy people in this world: stay away from them as their only interest is in getting YOU in trouble. You don't need any trouble in your life.

Netflix comedian, 'You' actor Chris D'Elia denies sexual misconduct allegations

The true definition of "pedophile: has sex with kids under the age of 11." So, he's technically not a pedophile. This girl has a gripe to get off her chest and it shouldn't be done PUBLICLY but that's Social Media for you: you have to be careful what you say these days. The sh*t's hitting the fan everywhere. It really is. What did he do to piss her off??? That's the real question.

The FBI called a powerful opioid developed for the military a public threat. The company selling the drug says it'll save lives.

"This was a drug that was a solution in search of a problem."
Steven Meisel, M Health Fairview: need I say any more about
what the government is going to do with ANOTHER drug that is
called Dsuvia and is "considered" a placebo: Hmmm: how's that
working out for you??? No matter what anybody does: there will
be addicts who will abuse the drug and end up killing
themselves (unintentionally, of course): alternatives to managing
chronic bone & muscle pain (neuropathy): 1. Yoga practiced
regularly 2. Ginger Root taken as a hot tea w/ lemon and non-
white sugar (honey or ???) 3. Clay Elixirs - look that one up
online and how to make it very easily - has to be taken at least 2-
4X per week 2 times per day - there are side effects w/ the heart
muscle, possible headaches: the upside of taking clay elixirs:
helps the bones & muscles to actually regrow themselves and
heal the pain point but you have to do this kind of healing for at
least 3 months, take a 2-3 day break then another 3 months of
healing - try a whole year then stop the healing and find out how
much better your bones and muscles feel-, ad infinitum. (I've
tried clay elixirs and they do work but you have to keep taking
them and just because you THINK you're getting better, don't
stop: that's where people go wrong w/ Natural/Alternative
Healing (roughly 38% of people believe in Alternatives to
managing their chronic pain issues). You have to keep doing
Natural/Alternative Healing like anything else you do like live
your life, take meds for problems (how much of Big Pharma
doesn't help the problem but gives you new problems - a vicious
cycle of "no end, no help" for body problems, etc. I'm sure that
if somebody has told you about something that will help your
"chronic pain problems" then by all means do some
RESEARCH before you try anything. "I'm not a doctor, so don't

sue me if you make your problems worse: I'm just THE MESSENGER." Sue yourself. The Hippocratic Oath: Do No Harm. RESEARCH any of the ideas I've dropped in this reaction. Go Now: do it for yourself or risk death with Big Pharma/the Government. It's your choice. Won't go any further about how "dangerous" medicine has become especially in this country w/ the CDC/Federal Government/Big Pharma, etc. Due Diligence = find out about the side FX, RX 1st then proceed to help yourself heal...it's all on you...

Adult film star Ron Jeremy charged with rape, sexual assault

"Will he get off at his trial???"

People are pranking their significant others with one sinister sentence: 'You could see the hurt in his eyes'

This viral challenge doesn't involve any planning at all — simply go up to your unsuspecting partner (or even a roommate or close friend) and tell them, "I feel like you could've been nicer to me today."

Maverick Ashley IN 3 SECONDS

Where's Doc Johnson when you need him to calm your emotions??? How about Samantha Sang from Australia who sang 'Emotions', or The Emotions who sang 'Best of My Love'??? What about them??? Or, Whitney 'So Emotional'. Hmmm... https://www.buymymainemadeartoday.blogspot.com

thanks so much: I'll put a SMILE on your face...

Jill Scott bewildered by plantations being turned into cozy getaway spots: It's like having a 'bed-and-breakfast at Auschwitz'

I don't care what Jill Scott's skin color is: that's not the issue: she just needs to shame people more about slavery: it ended in 1863 wasn't signed into law until 1865 by Abraham Lincoln. What's her point??? She needs more "face time". Could care less about that: just BLESS THE PLACE, i.e. "former plantation". I'm sure that some of the dead spirits are still hanging out there as that's what dead people do. Good Luck! A place can be repurposed for new life: that's how humans operate. Won't even touch the "slave trade" in other countries issue here. Not going there...

White actresses Kristen Bell and Jenny Slate vacate mixed-race voice roles: 'I am so very sorry'

I apologize for apologizing for apologizing for being sorry for doing something I was paid to do. I'm sooo...SORRY for being SORRY!!! Give me a break: how far are we going to take this apology shite??? I'm not buying into it...let's just get on a R E S P E C T each other like Aretha sang so long ago: can we just do

THAT???!!!
Taylor Swift Blasts US Census For Excluding Transgender, Nonbinary People

The world is full of bigots everywhere: IF you don't like somebody's SEXUALITY then keep your clap trap SHUT: it's really that simple: Diversity is the way to go: can't we all just get along??? Not in a million years: people like being bigoted - a person who is intolerant towards those holding different opinions: that's the way humans are: ALL people should be included in the Census as long as they're American Citizens...it's really THAT simple...got questions??? The Constitution guarantees our freedoms but frequently people who think they know it all will say otherwise because they're ignorant as the day is longer...go finger...

Country Stars Chase Rice, Chris Janson Spark Outrage With Videos of Packed Concert Crowds

The virus doesn't even exist as it's never been proven to exist: it's a scam and should be called Covid-1984 a/k/a 1984 - The Eurythmics or 1984 - George Orwell and it's exosomes that they're really talking about that turn into viruses: only .01% of the population dies from any virus: to read more about what Covid-19 PsyOp really is: https://www.toolsforfreedom.com go now: read up about this Psych Operation courtesy of the federal government.

The Nigerian Email Scammer

Who Stole Millions From Premier League Club, NY Law Firm, Banks

It's too easy to fall for any scam from anybody these days especially ADDICTS & people who pretend to be your friend(s): best thing to do is to keep your money tight like you know what and to say, "I'll think about it..." when anybody asks you for any money unless it's a LEGITIMATE TRANSACTION where you know you won't get ripped off: but, I have to say, "The whole world is a GIANT PONZI SCHEME designed to take your money from the grocery store, auto mechanics, banks, credit unions, insurance, lottery tickets, etc. etc." So BEWARE!!! The rich get richer and the poor stay where they're at: such a shame...

Rocker Ryan Adams Apologizes To 'This Is Us' Star Mandy Moore, Other Relationships For Abuse

If you are in an abusive relationship you can always choose to leave: if you stay you get more abuse, when you leave things change. However, if you come from an Abusive Family then it's harder to leave any relationship that is abusive. It takes time & commitment to get out of the b.s. Then when you move somewhere else thinking you've gotten away from the abuse then what happens??? More abuse: Solution: keep your friends close, your enemies closer and keep to yourself and stop repeating the pattern that got you there in the 1st place. It's up to Y-O-U to heal yourself. Do you deserve what you get??? It all ultimately is "Lessons On The Path of Life". Choose your life wisely, etc. You want PEACE, LOVE, LIGHT, HAPPINESS, ETC. Get the "Negativity Out of Your Life" and you'll eventually feel better. It just takes times.

Former Ellen DeGeneres Show Employees Claim They Were Subject to "Toxic Work Environment"

Nobody really knows what people are like until they meet 'face to face' and ACTUALLY WORK WITH THEM: until then NOBODY can say anything about that person: there are a lot of toxic people out there and your JOB is to IGNORE THEM: doesn't matter if they're rich or poor, fat or skinny, tall or short, etc. etc. YOU HAVE TO IGNORE THE CRAP THAT COMES OUT OF THEIR MOUTHS!!! It's just not worth listening to... https://www. finepopartinamerica.blogspot.com discover an amazing, talented Artist from Portland, Maine: go now...

Out of Portland tear gas, an apparition emerges, capturing the imagination of protesters

THE funniest thing I've seen all day longer: she's lucky she didn't get any pepper balls in her PRIVATE parts as that would have been VERY PAINFUL & POSSIBLY BLOODY!!! VERY LUCKY! https://www.fineartinamerica.blogspot.com go now...Collect some Art today...

Emitt Rhodes Dead at 70

You don't have to be FAMOUS to be a great pop lyricist/vocalist/musician/producer to be good at what you do: you just have to work at it all the time to get the traxx produced. Send e-mail:

ashleylenartson@yahoo.com & I'll send you one of my Produced traxx that somebody else sings and one of the Pop Jazz songs that I wrote and produced as a singer/master songwriter/lyricist: go now...

Judge denies release of teen girl who was jailed after not doing homework

The girl needs Pine Bark Extract to control her ADD/ADHD. As far as going to Juvy I wish I was 14 so I could go there and get laid. I know I'm being inappropriate but at least I'd get laid. HA! HA! HA! HA! HA! https://finepopartinamerica.blogspot.com Go Now...